HOW CAN I HELP

RORY
the
GARDEN BIRD?

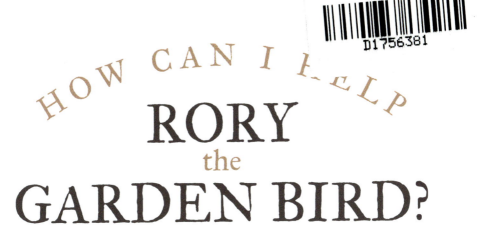

Frances Rodgers & Ben Grisdale

Editing, design and typesetting by UK Book Publishing

www.ukbookpublishing.com

ISBN: 978-1-8380019-2-6

HOW CAN I HELP

RORY

the

GARDEN BIRD?

Hello, my name is Rory,
I am a garden bird and I
need your help.

Let me visit your garden for food and water.

I like to drink and
wash in water.

Please give me a bird bath.

I like to eat bird seed mix
in the summer.

I like to eat fat balls
in the winter.

I also like to eat bugs and flies, so please plant flowers to attract them.

Trees are good for food and I
feel safe in them.

CAT
BELL

Please give me a home
in your trees.

Rubbish in your garden can
be a danger to me.

Please keep your garden tidy.

Please do not use
nets in your garden.

I can get stuck in them.

Please keep your bird feeders
and bath clean to stop me
getting poorly.

Thank you for all your help.

Now that you know how to help *Rory*, don't forget to help *Roly*, *Rosy* and *Roxy* too!

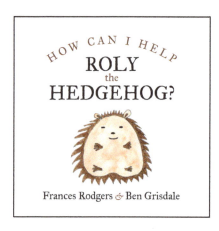

HOW CAN I HELP
ROLY
the
HEDGEHOG?

Frances Rodgers *&* Ben Grisdale

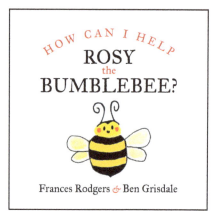

HOW CAN I HELP
ROSY
the
BUMBLEBEE?

Frances Rodgers *&* Ben Grisdale

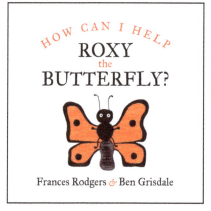

HOW CAN I HELP
ROXY
the
BUTTERFLY?

Frances Rodgers *&* Ben Grisdale

Available now on Amazon and other online retailers!

Lightning Source UK Ltd.
Milton Keynes UK
UKHW020823280920
370649UK00003B/11